Koupen-chan & You

RURUTEA

TUTTLE Publishing

Tokyo | Rutland, Vermont | Singapore

Hello!

Why I Wrote this Book

Five years ago, I became an illustrator and Koupen-chan was born. Simply put, this book is my reward for those past five years. Congratulations, Koupen-chan! Congratulations, me! When I was little, I thought I'd grow up to become a manga artist. I drew pictures every day and never got bored. But when I finally did grow up I ended up doing something completely unrelated—and thinking that was only natural. But here I am now, drawing pictures for a living! I was only able to do it thanks to my parents, who always praised my drawings, and my fans, who stood by me, and everyone who has supported me along the way. It seems I'm always on the receiving end! So let me once again express my gratitude: Thank you. I do hope you'll keep cheering for Koupen-chan's growth as a character and my own growth as an illustrator, because we've only just begun. And now I think I'll draw another picture, as a wish for happiness—happiness for me, and happiness for you, the reader of this book.

—Rurutea

You're amazing!

Here's an extra-big
spiral flower for you!

Don't forget to take a break.

Great job taking it easy!

Hooray! Hooray!
I know you got this!

Since today is
Valentine's Day...

I'd like to give you this!

Heh heh heh...

My name is Evil Enaga...!

Whadaya think of my Dark Jump move!?

Whoa!

What's happening!?

Heh heh heh... another day of training in the art of evil!

I'm awake...

I'm awa...
snore...

Morning, sunshine!
Geez, you look sleepy!

I made grub. Have some!

Today you get a spiral flower

just for eating!

Great job being kind!

Awesome job
challenging yourself!

You might be worried now,

but I know you,
and you'll do great!

You made it through the day!

How did it go?

Life's like that sometimes,
isn't it...

Let me pat your back
to cheer you up a little.

Go you! You brushed
your teeth this morning.

You are a gem!

Nice job pushing through
the sleepiness!

Getting stuff done on a
Saturday? You're amazing!

Warm
clothes →

It's cold today,
so bundle up, okay~

Go you!

You brushed your teeth
before bed.

Mmm...so warm...

Hug me

I'm warm!

Nice job preparing
for emergencies!

Good morning!
Want some pear?

I hear it hydrates your throat!

Nice! You aired out your room.

Smart move dressing warm!

Winter's creeping up on us.

Go you for staying on top
of your deadlines!

Just one more!

You must be tired from
working all night!

I brought you a pillow.
Take a nice long rest, okay?

Your spikes look quite nice
today, as always!

Evil Enaga! I found
a camellia on the street!

Me too!

Wishing you a safe day today,
and every day!

A gold star for you, hooray!

Just for waking up today!

Nice job stretching!

Recovery magic!

Hope you feel better soon!

Doing things the usual way

is good enough!

Wonder if there's a beetle
around here...

Yoo-hoo, Evil Enaga...

Heh heh heh...

Where are you?

Don't overdo it, it's hot today!

Good choice staying cool!

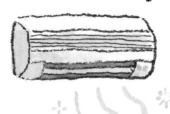

Beat back the scorching heat.

Smart move getting your vitamins!

Go you!
You washed your hair!

Go you for moving your body!

Nice, you're relaxing!

Have a mizu manju treat.

You ate breakfast!

I'm proud of you!

You're coming with me today?

Yippee!!

Good morning!
Have some water.

Go you for staying hydrated!

Hand towel

Smart move washing your hands.

I hope tomorrow
is a great day!

Here's your energy
recharging pillow!

Let's hang out at home. ♪

Welcome to Hanamaru Morning, the show that gets your day off to a fresh start! Well, we've passed the first day of summer! It's getting hot out there~

Welcome to Hanamaru Morning, the show that gets your day off to a heartwarming start! I've got a song request today from a certain Incarnation of Evil. Let's give "Read My Evil Mind" a listen!

Mmmh....

My eyes are so bleary...

Nice! You folded your pj's!

Go you for spending time at home!

How adorable...!

It's hot out, so don't overdo it~

Mmm, shaved ice.

Your bowl

Morning, sunshine.
How ya feeling?

Try to eat a bite or two.
You need the energy.

Good morning!
This is nice and cool.

Here, take it!

Oh, it's you! Good morning!

You're amazing for getting up
when it's so hot!

Today's the first day of fall.
It's still hot...

but after the Bon holiday,
it will start to feel more like autumn.

You're amazing!

You submitted your manuscript!

I'm taking away
your fever bit by bit.

I hope you're better
very soon!

Sweet dreams...

You rock for walking!

I hope your aches and pains
disappear soon!

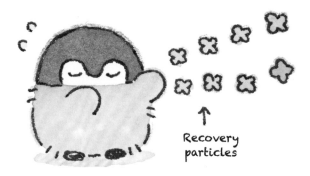

↑
Recovery
particles

You always work so hard.

Would you like a slice of this
quiche I made with Adelie?

Little by little,

you're growing up!

The older I get, the more
my adult charm blossoms!

Just kidding, ga ha ha

I'm here to take away
the humidity!

Heh heh heh..
Take a good look!

Isn't this outfit cool?

Heh heh heh...

I dug a hole to catch a foolish little bird!

Amazing...!

Go you for cleaning!

You went out in the rain?
You're amazing!

Good move getting some sun!

You started lifting weights again?
You're awesome.

Heave-ho!

We match!

Heh heh heh...

You worked hard this afternoon!
Would you like to relax and
have some rice crackers?

And some
tea!

Played too much yesterday.
Still sleeping.

Good morning!
Good choice sleeping in!

Today is my  birthday!

So...

I want to
give you this!

Let's have
some cake
together, too!!

You're all grown up now?

Cool!

Toot toot toooot! ♪

I always get sleepy when
I'm warm...

Everyone oversleeps

sometimes...

You got out of bed? Awesome!
Here's a spiral flower stamp!

spiral
flower
stamp

If you get enough stamps,
you get octopus dumplings!

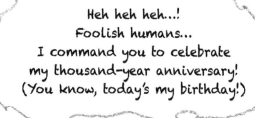

Another long day of doing evil...

Go me!
Heh heh...

I'm wearing a straw hat.

Heh heh heh...

← Favored cloak for cloak-and-dagger escapades

Go you!
You hung out your laundry!

Leave the dishes to me!

On Mondays,

you get a spiral flower just
for making it to lunch.

You got your body moving!

You're a star!

You got this.

Pat pat
You'll do great!

I'm proud of you!

You took a breath and
calmed down.

Nice job lining up!

It's starting to feel like spring...

Shrink! Even a tiny bit!

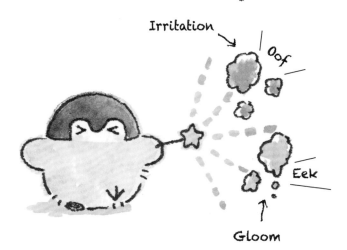

I'll take this for you.

Tickle tickle!

Are you awake now?

Hee hee, good morning!

I should take a bath soon...

Two hours later

Let's enjoy the
cherry blossoms together.

Good morning! Um,  let's have lunch together today.

And afterwards,  I, um...

... Never mind.  I'll tell you at lunch!

So, after lunch...

let's eat sweet
dumplings together!

We're cheering for you!

When you can't fall asleep,
you get a spiral flower
just for closing your eyes.

You planted rice?
You're amazing!

Rice is amazing!

Up we go!
Nice work out there.

Woosh

Hey! If you don't go to sleep, I'll have to make us some grilled rice balls!

Want a popsicle?

For you →

Good move eating lunch.

I'll join you!

Drool...

Oof! You're so strong!

You cooked!

Go you!

I brought something to help you pull through!

I made
ohagi rice cakes
for the equinox!

Ooh, those
look good!

Wanna eat them
with me, Rice Cake?

There's more in the kitchen,
by the way.

They're delicious!!
But somehow...

with a nickname like Rice Cake,
I can't help feeling guilty
eating rice cakes!

You drew this in 53 seconds?

You're so fast!

Nice work tidying up!

Go you for walking up a hill!

What do they call these
things again?

A belly
warmer?
Oh right—a
bellyband!

Where's
mine?

Here's one for you!
It's getting cold out there.

May you always stay healthy.

Recovery
from illness

I'm all soggy.

You dried your hair? Nice!

I dried mine a little too much.

I think the sky just took away
the last bit of summer...

Slowly but surely,
you're getting there...

I'm proud of you
for moving forward!

Morning, sunshine!
Eat some breakfast! Eat!

I made plain rice and chestnut
rice, which do you want?

Today's going to be a good day.

Today you get a spiral flower

just for getting up!!

Nice...job...resting....

Crab stick

Candy apple

Cotton candy

Candy plum

Heh heh heh...

Joy~

Drool...

Oooh...!

I'll be cooking,
so if you need me

just shout!

Don't overdo it, okay?

Remember, health is the source
of evil power...

I'll take away the bad stuff
in your body!

I hear kumquats are good
for your throat!

Have some!

Good morning!

Something good is going
to happen today!

Go you for doing the laundry!

Spin... spin...

You cleaned the tub?
You're awesome!

Thinking about which treat a friend would like best.

Go you for being thoughtful!

Amazing job studying!

I'm cheering for you!

Nice job bundling up!

I think I
overdid it.

Smart move

Watch
your step!

staying safe out there!

Always an early bird but
sleeping late today.

Good choice going to
bed early...

Polar Bear said they'd

take you to
work today!

Sometimes that happens.

Over
here!

I got a stollen from
the bakery!

Let's eat a little together
every day!

Good morning! Guess what?
Adelie said they'd
make a cake later!

Merry Christmas!
Here's a present from me to you,
dear friend!~♫

Go ahead, open it!

What are these for?

I'm drying some daikon radish and napa cabbage for pickles.

Great job!

That's it!

I wasn't sure how to put them in the barrel...

I don't wanna get out of bed...

You got out of bed!!
Go you!

You met your deadline?
You're amazing!

When you're not okay,

it's okay to say
you're not okay.

I'm putting a spell on you

so you won't get sick!

Are you okay?
Want me to carry you?

Are you sure you
can pick them up?

Someone said that to you?

You must have felt sad ...

I'll tell you enough kind things to make up for it!

You deserve thiiiis many spiral flowers!

I'll take the bad stuff way over here...

Look

I brought the speed-up key!

Instructions

① Wind wind...(?)

ba-dump
ba-dump

Round
it goes

② Whee!
I'm so fast!

Wow!

About
1.1 times
faster
than
before?

Hey...

What's wrong?

I'm a sucker for snacks!

So hot...

Ahhh

Nice job
getting your body
in balance!

This sauna sure is warm...

Smart move staying hydrated.

← Sports drink

I'm putting you somewhere
soft for a while.

Take a nice long rest, okay?

All that begins
must one day end.

That's why it's good to appreciate
what we have right now.

Mmm,
fluffy

I never thought
I'd see the day...

Are these yours?

I'll take them
for a while.

I'm just going to

soak them in some hot water...

Art by Evil Enaga

I'm here by your side!

Koupen-chan Gallery

Drifting...

Long-tailed tit
Japanese name: Enaga

Mochi dumplings...

Taiyaki

Drool....

Mame daifuku

My favorites!

Dorayaki

Joy...

Lemon

Lavender

Yuzu Honey

Soap

Adélie penguin

flipper

Back end when jumping

Fluffy...

King penguin

flap
flap

Chestnut season already...

Scarlet ibis feather

Okra

Sparrowhawk feather

Great spotted woodpecker feather

Secretary bird

Black-faced sheathbill

Japanese bantam female

Woodpecker foot

Eagle foot

KOUPEN–CHAN

HEH HEH HEH...

AMAZING!

\GO YOU!/

EVIL
ENAGA

Mole...

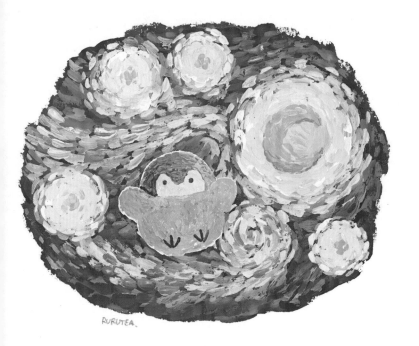

RURUTEA.

Oh my!

Munsell color model

Koupen-chan in the manner of Robert Delaunay's
Circular Forms

@Hankyu
Railway

@JR Osaka
Station walkway

@Banpaku
BEAST in
the Expo '70
Commemorative
Park, Osaka

@Carillon Plaza,
Osaka

@Pontocho,
Kyoto

@Kobe Port
Tower

@Matsuo-taisha Station

@Maruyama
Park, Kyoto

@Nakayamadera Temple, Takarazuka

Oh, it's you! Good morning!

I'm so happy to see you again!

"Books to Span the East and West"

Tuttle Publishing was founded in 1832 in the small New England town of Rutland, Vermont [USA]. Our core values remain as strong today as they were then—to publish best-in-class books which bring people together one page at a time. In 1948, we established a publishing outpost in Japan—and Tuttle is now a leader in publishing English-language books about the arts, languages and cultures of Asia. The world has become a much smaller place today and Asia's economic and cultural influence has grown. Yet the need for meaningful dialogue and information about this diverse region has never been greater. Over the past seven decades, Tuttle has published thousands of books on subjects ranging from martial arts and paper crafts to language learning and literature—and our talented authors, illustrators, designers and photographers have won many prestigious awards. We welcome you to explore the wealth of information available on Asia at **www.tuttlepublishing.com**.

Published by Tuttle Publishing,
an imprint of Periplus Editions (HK) Ltd.

www.tuttlepublishing.com

Koupenchan & You Koupenchan to ... ...
© 2022 Rurutea
English translation rights arranged with
SHUFU-TO-SEIKATSUSHA, LTD.
through Japan UNI Agency, Inc., Tokyo
Translation assistance by Ren (セイ蓮) @
koupenchan_yaku on X

ISBN: 978-4-8053-1929-1

28 27 26 25   8 7 6 5 4 3 2 1
Printed in China   2501CM

DISTRIBUTED BY

North America, Latin America & Europe
Tuttle Publishing
364 Innovation Drive
North Clarendon, VT 05759-9436 U.S.A.
Tel: 1 (802) 773 8930 | Fax: 1 (802) 773 6993
info@tuttlepublishing.com | www.tuttlepublishing.com

Japan
Tuttle Publishing
Yaekari Building 3rd Floor
5-4-12 Osaki
Shinagawa-ku
Tokyo 141-0032
Tel: (81) 3 5437 0171 | Fax: (81) 3 5437 0755
sales@tuttle.co.jp | www.tuttle.co.jp

Asia Pacific
Berkeley Books Pte. Ltd.
3 Kallang Sector #04-01
Singapore 349278
Tel: (65) 6741 2178 | Fax: (65) 6741 2179
inquiries@periplus.com.sg | www.tuttlepublishing.com